# Duck and the Balloon

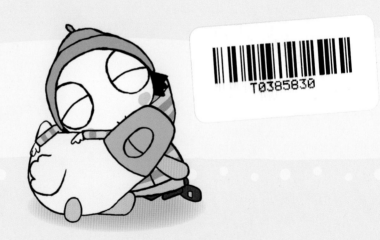

Adapted by Benjamin Hulme-Cross

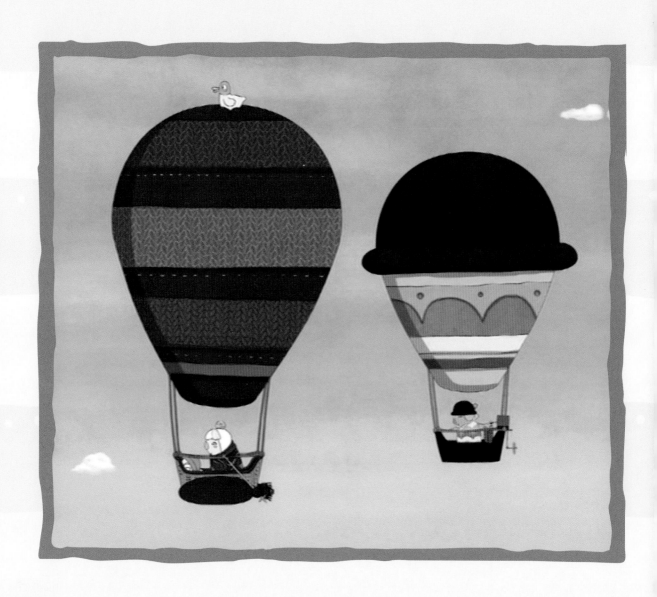

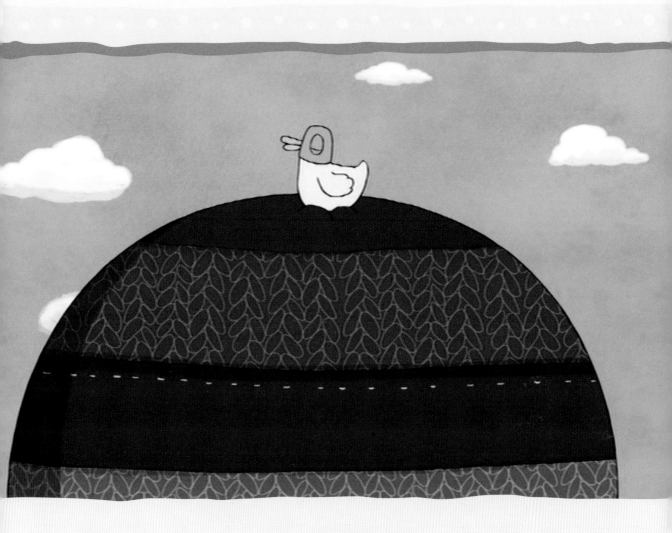

Duck is sitting on the big red balloon.

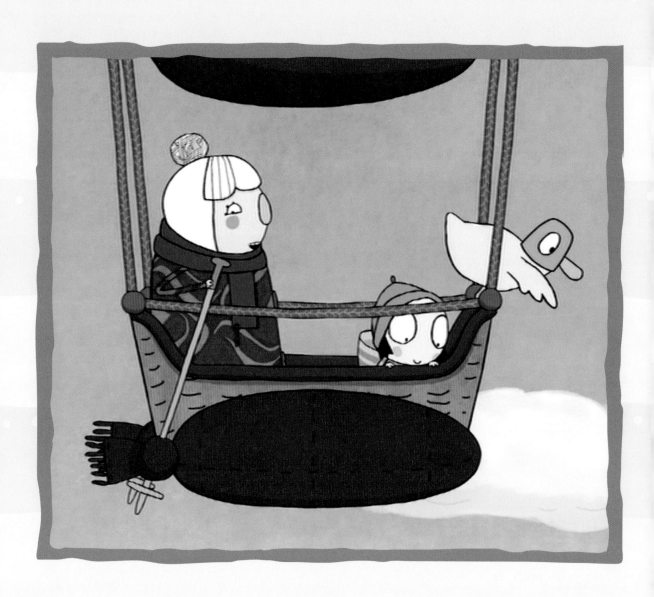

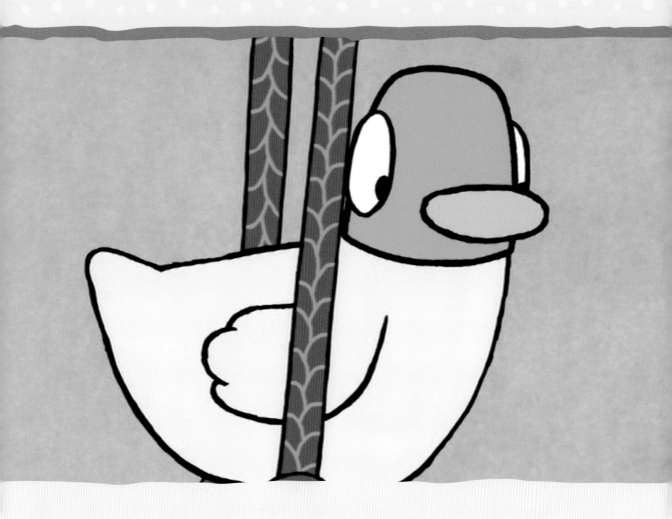

Duck is sitting in the big red balloon.

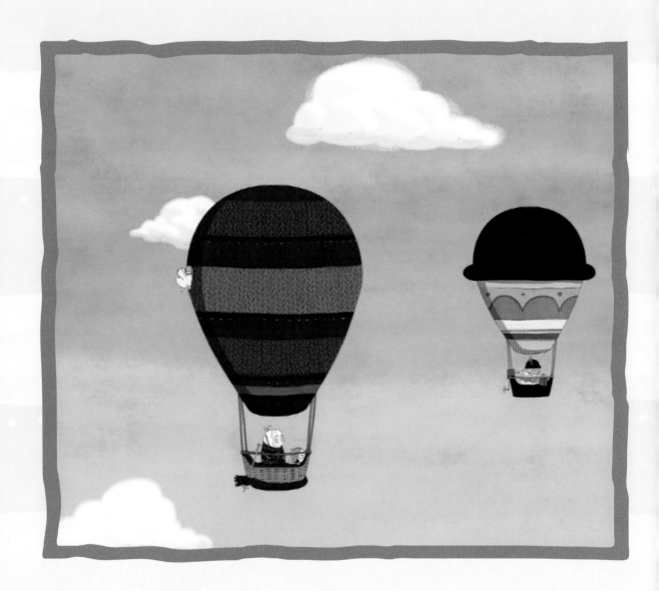

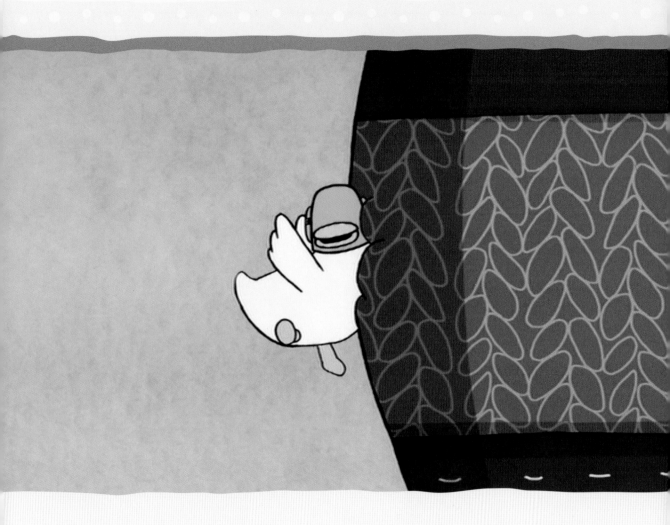

Duck is pushing on the big red balloon.

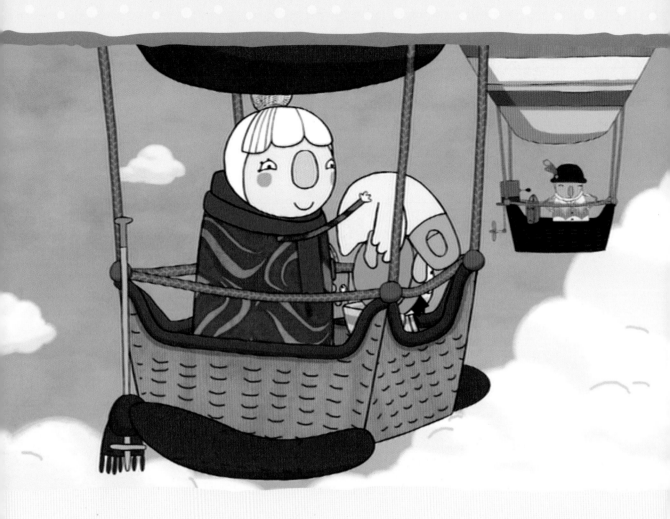

Duck is sleeping in the big red balloon